As If Labyrinth—

Pandemic Inspired Poems

As If Labyrinth—

Pandemic Inspired Poems

by

Jeannie E. Roberts

Cover design by Shay Culligan
Front cover photograph by Jeannie E. Roberts

ISBN: 978-1-954353-53-4

Kelsay Books
502 South 1040 East, A-119
American Fork, Utah, 84003

For Bruce & Andrew

Love is the bridge between you and everything.
—Rumi

Acknowledgments

My thanks to the editors and staff of the following publications in which versions of these poems have previously appeared.

Anti-Heroin Chic: "Song Sparrow"
Braided Way Magazine: "Merging with the Cosmos"
Chippewa Valley Writers' Guild, *The Hope Is the Thing Project:* "Hope Is the Thing That Repeats"
Piker Press: "Orisons for Our Front-Line Workers"
Quill & Parchment: "Evening Speaks with the Resonance of Trees"
Rye Whiskey Review: "She Bathes in the Watercolor Wash of Internal Light"
Sheltering with Poems, community & connection during covid: "Like Bloodroot, the Goodness in Humanity Rises"
Silver Birch Press: "At Our Local Family Fare's Guest Care Counter," "Even Now," "Feeling at Peace in a Field of Turquoise," "The Healing Garden," "Warriors Atop Pyramid B"
Synkroniciti Magazine: "As If Labyrinth, a Villanelle," "Reading the Sky at Sunrise"
The Ekphrastic Review: "The Process of Coping, Finding Peace in a World of Notions"
The Nervous Breakdown: "Coming to Terms with the Puzzle, Roller Coaster, and Happily Ever After"
The Poeming Pigeon, From Pandemic to Protest: "Your Case Number is 4783" (forthcoming, Fall 2021)
Trees in a Garden of Ashes, Poetry of Resilience: "When Eagles Reach Safety"
Verse-Virtual: "In Those Days, Humanity Followed the Stay-at-Home Mandate," "Unforeseen Winter"

Contents

Evening Speaks with the Resonance of Trees

Beyond the dock
booming sounds transmute the lake
its dissonance renders ice

reflections solidify
and the evening speaks
with the resonance of trees.

Perennials echo across a frozen landscape
stand resilient
where their inner rings resound.

Limbs lift amid currents
bow timbre within a draft
orchestrate the air as if a discourse, descant:

When weather governs be flexible
though remember your purpose
continue to rise.
Seasons of difficulty
become the instruments of growth.

Beyond the dock
booming sounds transmute the lake
its dissonance renders ice

reflections solidify
and the evening speaks with clarity.
Rooted in surefootedness

you step into strength
walk forward as you navigate the shoreline
resonate the resilience of trees.

Unforeseen Winter

Like a fever
the chapel chilled with disbelief
Shock rang
though work resumed

For months
fear consumed the average person
accelerated imaginations
unhitched society

still
the notion of spring
mellowed most
even those infected

Beyond the valley
where the virus was packaged
balloons and party favors
remained in the hands of politicians

As the days passed
some survivors burned their clothes
while others sat around the fires to mend

Unnatural as it was
no one spoke
yet bells were heard
easing
this unforeseen winter

Feeling at Peace in a Field of Turquoise

Somewhere, there's a mask, and somehow it was lost, left behind.
You tend to lose things, especially on walks—cram gloves
and hats into pockets, throw scarves over your shoulder,
though they slide, fall to frozen ground. Plodding across roads,

forging new paths, heavy boots as companion, you return home
overheated, beaded with the heartiness of cold weather exercise.
Once, you found your favorite scarf mangled by the snowplow.
You can't fix terminal loss. Still, you tried to mend it.

The mask you lost, left behind, was abstract, intangible,
sewn with interior stitches, yet, those with vision could see it.
Amid shadow, you stood before a windowed gathering,
watched people share ready conversation, easy interaction.

You weren't allowed to enter. Even so, you kept trying to pry
open the window. It's as if your insight sensed something
amiss, created a shield, an energetic field, protection from further
frostbite and judgment—as if you were being guided elsewhere,

away from the human condition, the downside of humanity.
You don't know. You *do know* the capabilities of the human
heart, its upside, generosity—the coronavirus has proven that,
for human beings have expressed compassion, united in goodness

and kindness, displayed courage and perseverance, as they help
others, risking their own lives in the process. What tangibles you
can't fix, like the scarf, you discard. What intangibles you *can fix,*
like the windowed gathering, you transmute into a brighter,

more unified manifestation, where humanity shines as an
integrated whole. Now, you wear a fabric mask, patterned with
peace signs and flower shapes, a pandemic gift made by your
neighbor. Somewhere, somehow, you lost, left behind, the mask

stitched with inner longings, the one patterned with grief, loss,
and panes of separation. Although, you continue to lose things,
overheat when you walk, you feel at peace, like a sea of Caribbean
hydrangea, patch of blue Himalayan poppies, where the scent
of lilac welcomes a field of turquoise.

The Pandemic Weight of Dreams, a Villanelle

Uncertainty leads to outlandish themes.
You've battled with monsters, fallen through ice.
Your nights include offbeat pandemic dreams.

You've noticed your jeans have torn at the seams.
Sweatpants expand for that extra cake slice.
Uncertainty leads to outlandish themes.

Savoring bites of éclairs filled with cream,
gluttony reigns as your number one vice.
Your nights include offbeat pandemic dreams.

You've tracked *Agent Orange,* led covert teams,
frightened *Boss Tweet* with your lexical spice.
Uncertainty leads to outlandish themes.

Eating, consuming with hypnotized gleam,
food is your fondness, not gambling or dice.
Your nights include offbeat pandemic dreams.

You've pounds aplenty, been startled by screams;
still, you're safe and well, not crawling with lice.
Uncertainty leads to outlandish themes.
Your nights include offbeat pandemic dreams.

She Applies Imagination in Times of Uncertainty

Near the pressed powder
next to the mascara
the one packaged in pink
she looks for her Raspberry Rush.
The cylinder brightens by the eyeliner
becomes a beacon beside the blush
where the concealer hides
as the tweezers glisten atop the 20x mirror.
She removes the cap
turns the case—
ah, the scent of fruit
and flower
lanolin
aluminum lake.
After inhaling its fragrance
applying its luster
she closes her eyes.
Lake Michigan shines.
It's spring in Door County.
The peninsula bursts with arctic primrose
cherry blossom
trailing arbutus
where lake iris gladden in lavender-blue.
She imagines this place—
then sees her mother
recalls her words as she lay in a hospital bed
have you found it, yet—my tube of lipstick?

Like Bloodroot, the Goodness in Humanity Rises

(Sanguinaria canadensis)

There's potentiality in the state of hesitation,
providence in delay. Living with wonder can shift
our focus to the importance of any given moment,

to the blink, the flash, the instant. As if veiled
in fatigue, held hostage in time, practicing gratitude
can lift our energy, release the feelings of suspension.

Like winter, the pandemic has placed humanity
in lockdown, a dark unknowing—
yet, there's opportunity in the interlude, the pause.

Our current hibernal yawn can unlock creativity,
lead to enlightenment, rebirth. Herbaceous
bloodroot accepts its interval, absorbs nutrients

without the urge to resurface, adjusts and grows
within its insular environment, where it ascends
anew. There's potentiality in the state of hesitation,

providence in delay. Living with wonder can shift
our focus to the importance of any given moment,
to the blink, the flash, the instant. Like bloodroot,

humankind has ever risen from the challenges
of existence. In times of uncertainty, the humane
collective awakens, cultivates renewal, reanimates
like spring.

Orisons for Our Front-Line Workers

when days become months
breathe fear and unease / blur amid virus
betray basic needs

pledge prayers of resilience / vitality / rest
repeat orisons / orisons / orisons
that bless

when days bestir doubt
befuddle belief / benumb gumption
bemire in grief

send grace to our nurses
true messengers of light / our doctors
heroes / warriors / knights

when days bewail loss
bemoan death and disease
befall illness / infection / befog inner peace

pledge prayers of resilience / vitality / rest
repeat orisons / orisons / orisons
that bless

Hope Is the Thing That Repeats

Waves shift
activate
appear
in intervals
like dominoes
flow
in a recurrent display.

As liquidity cycles
fractality unfolds
minerals rest
beneath buoyancy.

Encircled by atomic theory
and quantum mechanics
my hope recurs
in periodicity
as atomic orbitals
build
repeat
electron configurations.

In chemical drenches
and elemental curls
my molecular mass
attempts to fathom
the submicroscopic actions
of electrons in matter
here
my hope repeats
in predictable variations of marvel.

As If Labyrinth, a Villanelle

Spiders create silk from the spinneret glands.
Webs have existed for millions of years.
Insects are caught midst the gossamer strands.

Once, spiders fled from the water to land;
webs spun as protection eased primal fears.
Spiders create silk from the spinneret glands.

Threads contain protein, a spider web's brand.
Spiders move strings as if silk puppeteers.
Insects are caught midst the gossamer strands.

The sticky web fibers are flexible bands,
yet, tough as steel, nearly weightless and sheer.
Spiders create silk from the spinneret glands.

Like net, spiders weave an intricate plan.
Aerial traps are more efficient than spears.
Insects are caught midst the gossamer strands.

As if labyrinth, or the palm lines in hands,
its design is complex, like the innermost ear.
Spiders create silk from the spinneret glands.
Insects are caught midst the gossamer strands.

Even Now

with distancing rules and stay-at-home orders
finch
grackle
and blue jay still thrive—
launch from branches
wing to bird feeder
as crow lands
and wren evades window
sways
swerves
survives.
Even now
with face masks, cleaning, and handwashing guidelines
mink
muskrat
and otter still thrive—
glide across pond
dive beneath water
as frog leaps
and bass eludes snapper
sways
swerves
survives.
Even now
with mandates enforced and protocols applied
art
color
and luster still thrive—
beautify walls
dance across surface
as sun streams
and light dabs design

sways
swerves
survives.
Even now
in uncertain times with sweeping contagion
care
courage
and kindness still thrive.

Saving Painted Turtles

Look for the helpers.
You will always find people who are helping.
—Fred Rogers

Where cars hasten past the gate
race the diminishing light home
shells smash in a crimson array.
The road between ponds
bleeds plastron, weeps carapace.
The rampage of quitting time resembles
a throw caution to the wind
Jackson Pollock painting on blacktop.
Before the slaughter
you seek to rescue
Chrysemys picta.
At the very least
one can save turtles.
Cattails sway as catbirds call—
an applause for small efforts?
At times, they seem like futile ones
though not to the creatures gently lifted
placed out of harm's way.
Why not be a helper?
When a feather drifts
descends in subtle agreement
as if to say
"Slowdown be a helper, too."

When Eagles Reach Safety

Near the staghorn sumac
between the alder
and the bur oak
two Canadian geese
encircled by goslings
waddle beside the pond
and beyond the chain link fence
atop the electrical tower
a nest
charged with osprey
resounds
and past the weeping willow
above the canoe
where cattails rise
and red-winged blackbirds call
bald eagles travel toward home
and as they fly
crows gang together
chase tail feathers
until the white pine is spotted:

shalom.

The Process of Coping, Finding Peace in a World of Notions

Out beyond ideas of wrongdoing and rightdoing there is a field.
I'll meet you there. When the soul lies down in that grass the world is too full
to talk about.

—Rumi

at times
find yourself
where stillness
calm

you break away
elsewhere
floats
open

flee the path
in a field
is bright
bathed in light

while you're gone
with the notions
you're bright
though it fades

you course-correct
of this world
open
when

make peace
once again
bathed in light
you break away

flee the path
near a stream
is bright
bathed in light

find yourself
where stillness
calm
here

elsewhere
floats
open
you course-correct

like water
heal yourself
breathe
go back

flow with ease
love yourself
make peace
to the notions

find yourself
free yourself
try again
of this world

27

Warriors Atop Pyramid B

Columns of basalt rose unforeseen as if *P. strobus*
grew atop a plaster flat—here, in the Mexican state

of Hidalgo, sixty miles northwest of Mexico City,
amid a semi-arid climate,

breezes swayed your cotton dress in the ancient city
of Tula. Familiar with a continental climate

and the strong stance of Wisconsin white pine,
you were new to this Mesoamerican archeological

site and the stone sculptures that towered over you—
it was 1978, summer, when your twenty-one-year-

old self stood before a Toltec warrior. Five levels
of limestone, Pyramid B, Pyramid of Quetzalcoatl,

supported five warriors: four inanimate figures
with atlatls and an animate one with a camera—

though at the time, you'd no idea you were the fifth.

Coming to Terms with the Puzzle, Roller Coaster, and Happily Ever After

How do you synthesize what feels like nine lives, consolidate them
into one? Giant-sized puzzles take time to assemble, especially
jigsaws with four different *I do* plots.

Raised in the Barbie Cinderella era, unrealistic narratives skewed
your sense of reality. Grateful for your upbringing, girlhood
was cushioned with advantage: stylish clothing, summer travel,

pricey dinners at fancy restaurants. As if your early story
had been written in purple prose. After your father died, beige
replaced purple, perished like winter. Frozen in grief,

you opted for a new climate. Mired in make-believe, young
adulthood led you to Mexico City, where contrast offered
perspective. Here, you swept carpets with a broom, washed clothes

and dishes in a makeshift sink, lived sparingly amid the abundance
of Latin culture. Like imago, you emerged prematurely
from cocoon. For proper development, wings need stillness,

interval. Hurried flight can hinder growth. You've childhood
memories of a roller coaster, panic, airborne sensations.
It's nearly impossible to stabilize one's body with a broken lap

bar restraint. Perhaps this event was prophetic in its alarm,
for your heart boarded unchecked roller coasters, where wheels
spun on misaligned tracks.

Impaired orbits result in whiplash, muscle tension, and negative
g-forces. Yet, the repetition enhanced your courage, empathy,
and positive g-force acceleration, healed any generational

transference of trauma. Grounded in forgiveness and gratitude, like a cat, you've mastered the righting reflex; like an ancient lungfish, you've breathed water.

Why did you marry all of them? Are you crazy? Evidently, you're not neurotypical. Is anyone? Isn't humanity a mixed bag? Your chaos gave birth to a dancing star; after all, the hopeful,

idealistic non-conformist doesn't abandon the idea of fairy tale endings. Aligned, you ride smoothly, steer with internal approval, live happily ever after in self-actualization, for you trust

and honor your inner voice. Humankind's diversity is a giant-sized jigsaw puzzle, where all the pieces fit, are created equal. Assembly requires patience, honesty, and unconditional love.

Song Sparrow

(Melospiza melodia)

Trilling its notes with robust timbre, a song sparrow calls
from the limb of a silver maple. Below, near the shore, columbine
blooms, as does daisy, where nettles tower and a bull snake

weaves through the riverbank grape. Virginia creeper scales a pine,
as ashen clouds drape a morning storm. Still, the sparrow tilts its
head skyward, intones.

When you were fifteen, your father died of prostate cancer.
Like bird strike on a window, shock sent you tumbling down the
riverbank, careening toward a tangle of unknowns. Parental loss

before the age of twenty can impact adulthood in both obscure
and obvious ways. As your life unfolded, few guiding words
were expressed, though you recall—*Chin up. Smile.*

And, *kill them with kindness*—in response to oppositional forces.
It's not unusual for human beings to avoid uncomfortable
conversations, especially if the topic is death. When untethered

sensations manifest into feelings of displacement, can this
undercurrent reach solid ground? Your mother was a young widow
at forty-eight. You honor her tangle of unknowns,

have compassion and empathy for her journey. In her eighty-eighth
year she died and at ninety, she appeared as crimson columbine.
Her cremains remain a flowering perennial,

for she rises after Rush River's spring flood, where her presence
beautifies its eroded banks. As you approach your twilight years,
self-examination has accelerated, taken precedence.

How do you comprehend loss, the complexities of existence,
the maze, spiral, experience? Introspection is a worthy pursuit—
it can lead to enlightenment, appreciation, forgiveness.

Accepting what has shaped you is like a loving embrace.
When unpleasant subjects knock, speak with your children.
Transparency can build stronger relationships, invite the music

of connectedness. Revisions are ever available—the closed-door
dynamic can become the open one. When grief's sediment
descends, tilt your head skyward,

trill your notes across the heavens—sing. You are the brilliance
of a silver maple, merriment of daisy, vibrancy of a song sparrow
ascending above the ashen skies.

We Are One Lambent Body of Beautiful Diversity

By plucking her petals, you do not gather the beauty of the flower.
—Rabindranath Tagore

He who trims himself to suit everyone will soon whittle himself away.
—Raymond Hull

Her movements mirrored the slouch. Though unlike the collective,
she required more space. It was a new concept, the plus-size
model. Alongside the single-digit silhouettes,

she believed her stature appeared treelike, cumbersome,
as if an immovable structure, as it lumbered down the runway.
Oh, willowy world the forests and the woodlands also include

the oak, the pine, and the maple. In status quo style, the svelte
physiques dominated the catwalk. At the time, she was a novelty,
the square peg with the thicker trunk and branches,

the one who posed for *fat lady ads.* How could the common oak
thrive amid the wispy currents of the '80s? Narrow passageways
seldom nourished the wide stance of a keystone species.

Her figure was deemed upside down where it *should be* curvy,
topsy-turvy where it *should be* trim. And her expansive heart?
Diminished by the ongoing pinches, he called them *carnitas*

and sought leaner meat. After all, the totality of small chunks
of pork is equivalent to one large chop. Body-shamed,
she sharpened her whittle, encircled her hips and stomach

in cling wrap, wore a plastic sweatsuit, exercised to exhaustion,
and dropped the pounds. Eating disorders followed—size 4
was meant for willows, not for oaks.

Still, like the corrosive action in lithography, the stony stares
burned as the caustic remarks rocked her confidence. Perhaps
an intaglio, one incised with scalpel could guarantee favor?

As if chiseling away the excess could render a substantive life,
or filling the perceived inadequacies could land magic bullet
assurances. The willow's bark sap contains salicylic acid,

a medicinal aid for aches, fever, and pain relief. She couldn't
deny the elixir of experience. As if balm, a sense of calm
replaced her obedience to weight-based oppression.

A theriac in the form of compassion altered her perspective.
United in a lambent bond, sculpted with the hands of an unseen
force, the forests and the woodlands are a vast array

of harmonies, as is humanity. She dreams of the day *all people*
will honor the crown of diversity. Now, what rises from her deeply
rooted memories? She recalls the benevolence (the true shape

of beauty), the zest and camaraderie of performance, the jubilant
hub of artistic and creative expression. She scanned beneath
the surface, found the growth rings, absorbed its circles,
where the light had settled.

The TV, the Turtle, and Other Equal Measures of Variation

The places where water comes together with other water.
Those places stand out in my mind like holy places.
—Raymond Carver

Revealed at daybreak, a snapping turtle slogs up the bank,
an abandoned television tilts in disclosure. Mantles of pond residue
conceal their shells. The layers remind her of the cosmetic counter
clerks at high-end department stores, the stylish women

dipped in the products they sell. She recalls this life.
Dressed in a smile and brand name garb, she strolled through
Dayton's. Hired as a plus-size model, her physique was a hybrid,
double-digit one, an '80s crossbreed of amplitude and appearance.

She pauses from her walk, entertains the idea of moving both
the TV and the turtle. The electronic box is too heavy, so she
redirects her efforts, helps the snapper, offers it a safer path away
from the road. As if immersed in water, she revisits her years

in fashion, floats in the mixture of artistic sparkle and somber
sediment. Instinctive apprehension has shown her that external
contrast can evoke discomfort, especially when it's marked
by striking disparity.

There's as much radiance in the drab sturdiness of *C. serpentina*
as in the painted petiteness of *C. picta.* Despite the leavings
of belittlement, she remains bright, knows that amid any pool
she'll amplify as the hybrid, the empath, the thinker.

The settlings of experience have enhanced her insight.
She's yielded to narratives rife with pride, where servings of cold
shoulder became her existence. She understands the futility

of trying to change mindsets, prove your value. The actions taken
to gain acceptance result in exhaustion, create the kind
of heartbreak that spawns fear, shame, and isolation.

Like the TV, she's inhabited the fringes. Like the turtle, she's
slogged up the bank headed in the wrong direction. Yet, her inner
compass continues to wade through the debris, transmute the
darkness into sacred spaces.

Still, she wonders if global kinship is a possibility. Surely, it's *not
only* available in the denial of one's roots, in the obscurity of one's
light, or in the surrender to outworn conditions. And what about
the preeminence of bloodline, the import it carries?

Can alterity be welcomed into an established weave, embraced
with the same ease, interest, and enthusiasm? In the grander sense,
aren't we one in the collective of humanity? She observes
her surroundings, notices how beauty is expressed in equal

measures of variation, in the diversity of shapes, colors, and sizes.
Here, the holy places rise where the muskrat, the turtle, and the
wood duck thrive, *where water comes together with other water*
in universal belonging.

Thank You Letter to the Boy with a Defibrillator

The boy was born on a snowy
Thanksgiving morning.
He carried paddles
placed them on my chest
near middle mediastinum.

I heard the words / *CLEAR*.

The electric shock
reset my normal sinus rhythm.
Valves / atria / ventricles
resumed their cycle
began to beat
pump blood
deliver oxygen / nutrients
to a vital place—
my divine center.

Here
the restoration of purpose
cleared the way
for my maternal birth
where a wood thrush / cliff swallow
and meadowlark called
as if a beacon of light had warmed winter.

The boy was born on a snowy
Thanksgiving morning.
He carried paddles
placed them on my chest
near middle mediastinum.

I heard the words / *CLEAR.*

During defibrillation
as I pushed
my heart echoed
with life / love
and these words—
thank you, Son.

By Inner Leaps and Bounds

Inspired by an image of children stretching & leaping

The shamrock plants need watering, as do the baby
barrels. Mama cactus appears content,

for a dozen of her infants have been transplanted.
Together, her cacti family brighten the sunroom

in a ceramic pot. Their dirt nursery holds an array
of feathers. Blue jay, sparrow, and dove quills

stand in circular alignment. As if protective cradle,
I've taken them under my wing, feathered the nest.

Twelve feathers for twelve babies, my feather-fence
acts as a dreamcatcher—only good dreams

will do for this spiny brood. What we nurture,
nurture's us. The shamrock plants need watering,

as do the baby barrels. As if protective cradle,
I've taken them under my wing, feathered the nest.

There's euphoria in flight, watching the rise
of fledglings. The new growth prompts recollection.

Here, I envision, picture my body in motion—
bend my legs, lift my arms, take an inner leap—fly.

Merging with the Cosmos

mid-morning in the overcast slate stillness
near broken sticks
and jagged rocks
where lake water ripples
and driftwood lands
you hear the lamentation of doves
the caterwaul of catbirds
the metallic resonance of blue jays
as grackles wing in ruler-straight swiftness
where squirrels scale a locust
an ant zigzags
as cardinals call beside the featherlike fall
of cottonwood
here
cosmos display ochre and yolk
where you merge amid the universe of blossoms
observe your existence
hold physicality in contemplation
as you spin within the space-time continuum
in the overcast slate stillness of morning

Kayaking During the Pandemic, a Villanelle

There's a loon alert heed on Henneman Lake,
it's a safety request, one more for the times,
posted left of the landing beside leafy brake.

The notice is bold, nailed to thick, wooden stake:
keep loons safe on the water, free near divide.
There's a loon alert heed on Henneman Lake.

This warning, as others, is valid not fake.
In John-Deere-yellow, it's a well-designed sign,
posted left of the landing beside leafy brake.

Loons float together, a gathering of mates,
we observe from afar, in awe as they glide.
There's a loon alert heed on Henneman Lake.

We adhere to the tenets of our fair state,
honor the distance-and-well-being guidelines,
posted left of the landing beside leafy brake.

We bow to all life, its diverse forms and shapes,
praise Earth, nature, and the whole of mankind.
There's a loon alert heed on Henneman Lake,
posted left of the landing beside leafy brake.

Henneman Lake is located in Chippewa County, Wisconsin, USA

She Bathes in the Watercolor Wash of Internal Light

After an image by Charles Dana Gibson
(American Illustrator, 1867–1944)

Your somber mood and sloping cigarette
may pair well with the favored cocktail of your creator—
though, gin garnished with pickled onion is an acquired taste.

Gibson Girl,
you appear weary as you pose in inky nonchalance.
Do your arms shield you from darker orbits?

One day,
the barrier between you and everything will dissolve—
perhaps you'll awaken in a watercolor wash,

slides of blush, streams of coral,
where tangerine meadows flow near spills of pastel,
as slips of subtlety move toward internal light.

Even pen-and-ink lives,
linear narratives,
can render softness,

when focus buoys
with eyes at center,
where sentience is breath.

Blessed Are the Inks of Alchemy

Inspired by a painting of the number eight

Neither prime nor semiprime, though lucky
you shape the gateway to infinity.
As if the Beatitudes buoy above the crown
embed blessings in the soul star chakra
where subtle energy unlocks the portal
to grace, somewhere between blue
and green, somewhere inside the grains
of sand and sermon, enlightenment
awakens the sleepy ways of humanity
and optics reveal the kingdom, hold clarity
in eights, in the inky alchemy of the artist's vision.

Envisioning Inclusion for the Ones Who Float

Otherness floats with the whispers of breeze,
joins the reverie of clouds, muses with the scent of pine,
where the wariness of ravens convene in insularity.

After decades, you return with optimism, anticipate
acceptance, foresee change. Though contentment
appears to thrive on the preservation of the status quo,

the practice of othering, the storytelling of ravens.
Here, the wand of resistance directs existing conditions.
Holding your rose quartz, you envision inclusion,

imagine light; an amplifier; a compass; an ocean;
and an eraser. The light surrounds the margins with hope.
The amplifier boosts the marginalized voices with confidence.

The compass offers guidance, clarity, and a sense of safety.
The ocean flows over the island, makes peaceful waves,
blends kindness with the feelings of belonging.

The eraser removes the rust, cleans the slate,
where the chalk is ready to write balanced equations,
author new narratives. The rose quartz radiates trust,

transmutes fear into universal love. Now angels hover,
transmit empathy, distribute peace, ascend with the company
of ravens. After decades, you realize why you've returned:

to practice equality, to sway the welcome wand, to champion
the ones who float with the whispers of breeze, the reverie
of clouds, and the scent of pine needles.

Learning from Asiatic Lily

There can be no lotus flower without the mud.
—Thich Nhat Hanh

As the red lick of sunrise brightens the air
you stand near sheets of greenery
pause beside pillows of hosta / moss
witness / where love lands to kiss lilium lips.

Slick with dew / petals glow
as tongued bowls greet wasp
answer beetle / respond in kind.
You / too / were once kissed
warmed in morning light.

Here / emotions drift / shift
as you sort through memory
contemplate love's complexities.

Like panning for gold
extracting aurum from pyrite
authenticity from tinsel
truth from falsehood
you've come to believe:
there can be no lotus flower without the mud.

Perhaps the embodiment of love
resembles our natural world
fleeting moments / small offerings
energetic nectar / filling / emptying our bowls
like the seasons / where flow exists
without expectation / push of promise.

In this perennial garden
color reaches with the scent of invitation
vibrancy holds lessons of living in the now
urges us to release the past
embrace our significance
illuminate the air with strength / acceptance / like Asiatic lily.

Reading the Sky at Sunrise

first light seeps indigo / inks apricot
pens peach / *honor the Earth* / sky
scriber speaks / *guard as if gold*
manage with care / stanzas sing pink
syllables shape air / first light forms
amber / lines cinnamon / frames rose
see verse afloat / *read world as poem*
honor the Earth / sky scriber speaks
tidings of truth / epistles of peace

In Those Days, Humanity Followed the Stay-at-Home Mandate

Confinement aided in the COVID-19 'Flatten the Curve'
campaign, still

Osprey, lesser scaup, and other migratory waterfowl arrived,
as did spring

relationships changed, some deepened

Others became increasingly distant, though connection
through technology bridged the gap

navel-gazing, bird-watching, mask-making,

and "couch-potatoing" rose, along with arts and crafts

Vacations were forbidden

isolation and social distancing were the key protections
in trying to control the pandemic

restrictions were important, standing six feet away from people
saved lives

Unity through uncertainty

Strengthened society, and the world pulled together figuratively
while remaining physically apart

Remember the Loons, a Villanelle

For Bruce, on his 65th birthday

Remember the loons on Henneman Lake.
Together, we paddle along the shoreline.
We hear a song trio, juvenile plus mates.

It's a pristine setting, natural not fake,
where lily pads float and clear water shines.
Remember the loons on Henneman Lake.

Three bellies propel with aquatic bird traits,
dive beneath surface, ascend near white pine.
We hear a song trio, juvenile plus mates.

Four otters cavort, then make their escape.
We watch these creatures as they intertwine.
Remember the loons on Henneman Lake.

We kayak past frogs and riverbank grape,
by turtles, cattails, and ducks in a line.
We hear a song trio, juvenile plus mates.

Moments in nature can soften the aches;
it's a lifegiving gift, restorative time.
Remember the loons on Henneman Lake.
We hear a song trio, juvenile plus mates.

Henneman Lake is located in Chippewa County, Wisconsin, USA

At Our Local Family Fare's Guest Care Counter

The pandemic may have altered our way of life,
still, there's familiarity inside our local grocery store.
Even with mask wear, we smile,

extend the light of kindness.
Today, USPS Frog Forever® Stamps are on my list.
As I stand in line, I admire how the guest care clerk,

Christena, works and interacts with poise.
"Hi, how's your day going?" I say,
then ask for my beloved croakers.

Muffled chuckles rise from beneath the clerk's mask.
My enthusiastic request for frogs
must have struck her funny bone. I laugh, too.

Next, I walk toward the greeting card section,
where I take my time selecting birthday, anniversary,
and thinking of you sentiments.

I can't imagine an existence
without the United States Postal Service.
Its beginnings date back to 1775

when Benjamin Franklin became the first postmaster general.
For years, my brother worked at the South 1st Street post office
in downtown Minneapolis.

People depend on postal jobs for their livelihood.
Determined, I head back to the counter,
buy two more sheets of postage,
including the USPS Women Vote Forever® Stamps.

Once again, I thank Christena for her frontline dedication
as I envision Joe and Kamala
by my side
with the same fondness for amphibians
and the 19th Amendment to the U.S. Constitution.

Your Case Number Is 4783

A case number has been assigned to your loved one
and will appear on the waiting room monitor, so you can follow his or her
progress through surgery. To protect privacy, no names are used.
                                        —Mayo Clinic Health System

You see green. Your eye awaits slate, the last of the seven stages.
Masked and six feet apart, you sit with the other primary patient
representatives. Between screen glances, you crochet.

The lady across from you knits. You're crocheting a hat for your
son. She's knitting a scarf. You admire her project, are curious
to know if it's also a gift. In synchronized production,

we move our hands like spiders' weave webs. We've established
an energetic connection—the generation of each row soothes
our angst, nourishes our being. The vigor of creation, its axial,

repetitive motion, streams internal peace. In steady focus,
you activate the yarn, rotate the fibers around your left index
finger, turn the needle with your right thumb, index and middle

fingers. Together, yet distanced, we perform manual operations,
build something from scratch. As the strands loop and twine,
you envision the thoracic surgeon, his team, harvest veins;

attach blood vessel grafts; shape a life-giving labyrinth; restore
the myocardium. It's in our nature to be heart-centered, to create
with the vital currents of our essence. After a quick monitor check,

you scan the color-code card supplied by one of the front desk
assistants. Shades of blue are forthcoming, a buoyant indication
of calm seas, clear skies.

Here, you revisit the colors that represent the seven surgical steps:
(1) pale yellow—in facility; (2) sunflower yellow—pre-procedure;
(3) rust—procedure; (4) emerald green—procedure start;

(5) cobalt blue—procedure close; (6) sky blue—recovery;
and (7) slate—complete. You watch the knitter, imagine her life,
petition prayers for her loved one.

Could she be visualizing the progress of a similar off-pump
procedure? If so, you wonder how many coronary arteries
will be bypassed, one, two, three, four? Could it be five,

a quintuple, like your husband? When suddenly she gathers
her things, places the scarf and skein in a bag, stands, and smiles.
She must have seen slate.

The Healing Garden

is my sanctuary. It's just down the hall from the critical care unit.
I open the door and see a poem—

sansevieria rises near the sturdy stalks of yucca. Dieffenbachia
thrives atop the limestone divide.

Down the pathway, a Christmas cactus appears like an umbrella,
a sage-green, welcome sentry to the meditation area.

I walk toward the bench, sit in the same spot my husband sat
the afternoon before his quintuple bypass surgery. That day,

vivid in my mind, a ray of light slipped through the vaulted
ceiling of glass. I have faith in signs—this one radiated

with therapeutic expression. Nearby, the "Believe" fountain
cascades in gentle succession. How can an active, athletic guy

need new arteries? The prognosis was put this way: *You're one
blood cell away from having a massive heart attack.*

Besides the plants, the waterfall, there's artwork. Ceramic tiles
by local artists grace the walls. Caradori dragonflies and cherry

blossoms dance near the lilac beauty of LeAir iris, as a Balwierz
seascape softens next to the orange swirl of Marrs's koi fish.

My haven also cultivates cabbage, though not your typical variety.
This kind is spelled with a capital C, capital A, capital B,

and a capital G, the acronym for coronary artery bypass graft.
Yes, I do believe in the "Believe" fountain, for it flows with life-
saving miracles.

Deep Gratitude

for our health-care professionals, to the thoracic surgeons, the surgical team, and the entire medical staff at the Mayo Clinic, Luther Campus, Eau Claire, Wisconsin, USA. My husband's CABG was performed on September 4, 2020, during the Coronavirus Pandemic.

*

for my husband, Bruce, his gifts of companionship, consistency, and creative time, for my son, Andrew, his gifts of motherhood, inspiration, and unconditional love.

*

for my father, Donald, my mother, Karin (Alice), my brother, Steven, my sister, Mary, for my relatives, ancestry, and for the opportunity to have experienced other family units, including stepfamilies.

*

to the friends, mentors, poets, editors, and publishers who have shown support and enthusiasm for my poetry, who have assisted in my literary development, and embraced my work in some way along the path of my writing career, in alphabetical order: Linda Aschbrenner, Cynthia Atkins, Gene Barry, Deborah J. Benner, Ed Bennett, Ron Bergin, Kristy Bowen, Jack Bushnell, Sarah Sadie Busse, Jane L. Carman, Jan Carroll, Kai Coggin (including her online series Wednesday Night Poetry Virtual Open Mic, Poetry Through the Pandemic and its participants), Karen Kelsay Davies, James Diaz, Norma Desprez's critique group, The Porch Poets, and its participants, Julian Emerson, Firestone Feinberg, Max Garland, Penny Harter, Candace Hennekens, BJ Hollars, Holly J. Hughes,

Andrea Janda, Ginny Kaczmarek, Dean Kallenbach, Erna Emmighausen Kelly, Mehtab Khalsa, Christen Kincaid, Peg Carlson Lauber, James E. Lewis, Sandra Lindow's critique group, the L. E. Phillips Memorial Public Library Writers' Group, and its participants, Lorette C. Luzajic, Leah Maines, Betsy Mars, Gary Mazzone, Diane M. Millis, Kate Mulvaney, Joe Murphy, Cristina Raskopf Norcross, Jessi Hoy Peterson, Meredith Pirazzini, Saara Myrene Raappana, Michelle Messina Reale, Paige Riehl, Brian and Sue Roegge, Lin Salisbury, Rachel Shields, Beate Sigriddaughter, Tricia Quirk Spitzmueller, Jason Splichal, Nadine S. St. Louis, Alison Stedman, Sharmagne Leland-St. John-Sylbert, Bruce Taylor, Melanie Villines, Joanne Vruno, Bill Yarrow and others.

About the Author

Jeannie E. Roberts has authored four poetry collections, including *The Wingspan of Things,* a poetry chapbook (Dancing Girl Press, 2017), *Romp and Ceremony,* a full-length poetry collection (Finishing Line Press, 2017), *Beyond Bulrush,* a full-length poetry collection (Lit Fest Press, 2015), and *Nature of it All,* a poetry chapbook (Finishing Line Press, 2013). Her second children's book, *Rhyme the Roost! A Collection of Poems and Paintings for Children,* was released in 2019 by Daffydowndilly Press, an imprint of Kelsay Books. She's also the author and illustrator of *Let's Make Faces!,* a children's book dedicated to her son (author-published, 2009). Her work appears in North American and international online magazines, print journals and anthologies. She holds a B.S. in secondary education and an M.A. in arts and cultural management (arts administration). In 2007, her poem "La Luz" won first place in the Green Bay Symphony Orchestra's statewide poetry contest. Musical composer Daniel Kellogg set her poem to music via an orchestral score with choir. In 2008, this new work was performed by the Green Bay Symphony Orchestra with the Dudley Birder Chorale. Born in Minneapolis, Minnesota, she's listed in the Poets & Writers Directory, is a member of the Wisconsin Fellowship of Poets, and is the poetry reader and editor of the online literary magazine *Halfway Down the Stairs.* When she's not reading, writing, or editing, you can find her drawing and painting, outdoors photographing her natural surroundings, taking long walks, listening to the birds, and identifying plants and flowers. Roberts is an animal lover, a nature enthusiast, and an equal rights advocate.